CARING FOR THE FORESTS

Written by
Azra Limbada

BookLife
PUBLISHING

©2020
BookLife Publishing Ltd.
King's Lynn
Norfolk PE30 4LS

All rights reserved.
Printed in Malaysia.

A catalogue record for this book is available from the British Library.

ISBN: 978-1-83927-255-4

Written by:
Azra Limbada

Edited by:
John Wood

Designed by:
Drue Rintoul

All facts, statistics, web addresses and URLs in this book were verified as valid and accurate at time of writing.
No responsibility for any changes to external websites or references can be accepted by either the author or publisher.

PHOTO CREDITS

Images are courtesy of Shutterstock.com. With thanks to Getty Images, Thinkstock Photo and iStockphoto. Cover – Jackal Yu, zlikovec. 4&5 – Denis Tabler, Dudarev Mikhail. 6&7 – Smileus, Fotos593. 8&9 – Monkey Business Images, atiger. 10&11 – Papa Bravo, Tilo G. 12&13 – ALPA PROD, Thep Photos, Tyler Olson. 14&15 – Jay Ondreicka, Sumala Chidchoi. 16&17 – Peter J. Wilson, Soloviova Liudmyla. 18&19 – Rasta777, ZayacSK. 20&21 – Mike Jett. 22&23 – Pong Danviboon, Butsaya, Liz Kcer, kozirsky, Andrey Solovev, ConstantinosZ.

CONTENTS

Words that look like <u>this</u> can be found in the glossary on page 24.

EARTH

We live on Earth. Our planet is about 4.5 billion years old. It is home to all sorts of living things. Life can be found everywhere, from steamy jungles to dry deserts.

WHAT CAN YOU SEE?

Can you see how green the grass is?
Can you see the tall, wavy trees?

FORESTS

A forest is made up of lots of different trees. Many animals live in forests and need them in order to stay alive.

The Amazon is the largest rainforest in the world. A rainforest has lots of rain every year. There are millions of different <u>species</u> living in the Amazon.

OXYGEN AND CARBON DIOXIDE

Oxygen is all around us. It is a colourless <u>gas</u> that we need to stay alive. Every time we breathe in, we are taking in oxygen. Plants and trees make oxygen.

Carbon dioxide is in the air that we breathe out. Trees and plants need carbon dioxide to grow. This means animals and plants rely on each other.

OXYGEN

CARBON DIOXIDE

WE NEED THE TREES AND THEY NEED US!

LIVING IN THE FOREST

Did you know that lots of people live in forests too? These people rely on trees and forests for their food and shelter.

Animals also need the forest to live. Animals such as sloths and monkeys use tall trees for shelter and to hide from their predators.

SLOTH

TREES

We use trees for lots of things. Wood from trees can be used to make houses. We also get lots of our medicine and food from trees.

Paper is also made from trees. The more paper you use, the more trees are cut down. This is why it is important to recycle your paper.

PEOPLE MAKING PAPER

DEFORESTATION

Deforestation is when trees in forests are cut down. Cutting down trees without planting new ones is bad for the <u>environment</u>.

You can help stop deforestation by being responsible and reusing things that are made from trees, such as paper and card.

FOREST FIRES

A forest fire might be started by something in nature, such as a lightning strike. However, most forest fires are caused by humans.

Forest fires destroy habitats and add to the pollution around us. Sadly, it often takes a long time for a forest to recover from a fire.

FOREST FIRES ARE OFTEN CAUSED BY CAMPFIRES. REMEMBER TO ALWAYS BE SAFE WITH YOUR CAMPFIRE!

MINING

Mining is when humans dig deep into the ground to get things such as metals and coal. Coal is used to make electricity, but it causes lots of pollution.

Lots of trees are cut down before mining can happen. Mining can also pollute the ground or water nearby, killing even more plants and trees.

ISRA HIRSI

This is Isra Hirsi. She is an <u>activist</u> who is trying to stop <u>climate change</u>. Isra wants everyone to work together to help protect our planet.

Isra speaks at lots of protests. A protest is a large group of people who get together to show a dislike of something, such as climate change, to try and make a difference.

MAKE YOUR OWN RECYCLED WIND CHIMES

Here's everything you need to make your own recycled wind chimes.

STEP 1: Paint the outside of your cans. Once they are dry, ask an adult to make a hole in the bottom of the cans.

STEP 2: Push your string through the hole.

STEP 3: Tie some washers along one end of the string, inside the cans. They will hold the string in place and make noise.

STEP 4: Hang the cans outside using tape. When the wind blows, they will make a lovely sound.

GLOSSARY

<u>activist</u>	someone who tries to make a change by speaking out
<u>climate change</u>	a change in the typical weather or temperature of a large area
<u>environment</u>	the natural world
<u>gas</u>	a thing that is like air, which spreads out to fill any space available
<u>habitats</u>	the natural homes in which animals, plants and other living things live
<u>pollution</u>	when something is added to our environment that is harmful to living things
<u>predators</u>	animals that hunt other animals for food
<u>recycle</u>	use again to make something else
<u>rely</u>	trust or depend on something
<u>species</u>	a group of very similar animals or plants that can create young together

INDEX